Dearest Lord, When Will I Die?

by

Peter Francis Pegnall

Dearest Lord, When Will I Die?

First published 2019 by The Hedgehog Poetry Press

Published in the UK by
The Hedgehog Poetry Press
5, Coppack House
Churchill Avenue
Clevedon
BS21 6QW

www.hedgehogpress.co.uk

ISBN: 978-1-9164806-1-2

This collection is dedicated to Mind; to Turning Point; to my fellow survivors from Hartley House, especially Pat Cassidy; to the extraordinary workers in The NHS and to my very funny friends in AA. Without whom, nothing...

Many thanks for the editorial clarity and sensitive acumen of Jane Draycott.

Contents

like willie loman I favour gardening at odd hours 9

1862: Three Hundred and Sixty Six Poems. 10

I do not know why Miss Dickinson dreaded that first robin 11

Lifelines 12

Home 16

Applause, King Lear 17

Suffer 18

Back to Nature? 19

Dancing on different shores 20

blood red moon 23

Bees and Candles 24

I'm Ready for my Close Up, Mr. De Mille 27

I am a Tibetan Buddhist, ... 28

Inarticulate Speech of the Heart, or How Karlowicz Wrote About
His Friend's Suicide 29

Crows and Chimpanzees are of equal intelligence 30

The lamb who watched television and the cow who got in a mood.
.... 32

TripAdvisor 33

One of the best. 34

Elegy for Mankind at the Sea Side 35

A bird that sings on and on, late into the season, is probably a
lonely bachelor who has failed to attract a mate 36

The strangely vacant gaze of the fishmonger's wife 37

I've just heard Richard Rodney Bennet Play 'The Man I Love' . 38

A Penny for Them 39

Nothing is that funny (for Gerald) 40

Hidden shallows 42

Little Boxes 43

Melancholia 44

I met a traveller from a modern land 45

Ages of Uncertainty 46

Dance Music 49

Harp Craft 50

Audenesque 51

Dearest Lord, When Will I Die? 52

LIKE WILLIE LOMAN I FAVOUR GARDENING AT ODD HOURS

usually in my candy striped trunks;
unlike poor, repulsive, deluded Willie,
I have more than a square of concrete,
at least for now. When I gaze upward,
I catch puffy marshmallows as they float
and luxuriate; I hear the North Sea groan,
I trouble a pair of doves in the cypress,
I pad barefoot on the springy turf.

This is the life. I send a postcard
to myself saying so, wishing I were here.

1862: THREE HUNDRED AND SIXTY SIX POEMS.

A poem a day keeps the - nothing
away- her detonations
not so much as twitched the net
at the window - defied salvation

in hymnal rhythms - You'd never catch
 her drift, not if you ebbed on the shore
like seaweed in her ceaseless surge -
the less she held secure - the more-

Do Not Disturb outside the room -
as if we could - all present
and correct - Emily unbalanced -
bent on decomposing what we think she meant

I DO NOT KNOW WHY MISS DICKINSON DREADED THAT FIRST ROBIN

(for Billy Collins)

unless it was her usual way of being special
of taking ordinary folk by surprise
with a perversity iridescent
a daring so calm

unless she cracked on until she could find
a way into the next line that almost
made sense- then withdrew- neatly-
oh the needlework of the soul

unless the fabulous patchwork of nature
seized her small frame- discomposed
her like first love or last breath
and she saw only blood on her pinafore

sacrifice in sight. Queen Emily
she's my friend she allows me anything
but to remove her clothes- one by one-
she has done so already.

LIFELINES

(for Padraig and Sophie)

1.

A bird in flight can lift our spirits
higher than we know how to climb.

That same bird, on reflection,
dives deep inside, where it hurts and heals.

2.

Here is everything needful
for a crucifixion.

Except for the timber
and the nails.

Except for the soldiers
and the baying crowd.

Except for the weeping women
and darkness over all the earth.

Here is more than adequate
here is the whole story.

Except for resurrection.

3.

Perhaps if I sit here long enough
I shall take root, I shall mine
sustenance and life after life
in the earth.

I shall sift light and shade
among my leaves, bend with the breeze,
harbour the crow and the termite,
net the moon on its nightly flight.

Reserve epitaph for the dead.

4.

My windpipe thickens
with still born cries
mouth stitches silence
through a quilt of days.

Meanwhile, a seven year old
beats her brain against
the battle cries of consonants
tumbles down a whirlpool of vowels.

Surfaces, bright and wide open
as a field of buttercups,
already on the next page,
as yet unwritten.

HOME

a warm sound, that closes in on itself,
a yearning, a place to begin and end;
somewhere lost before it can be found.

I'd drag my heels on the way back,
walk the last two bus stops, skip the cracks
on the grey pavements, count the steps.
Not in fear, not in rebellion. My own time,
my shape to carve in the gathering dusk;
you never knew what the closed door held.

Books were the passport to my own country:
reckless heroes, snazzy villains, outlaws,
shameless and free, for a while. In a town
ruled by men who took their belts to their sons,
who barked intolerance like bull terriers;
by women who served out guilt with Sunday dinner,
who wept and laughed and yelled and kept silent-
never ending switchbacks that cost the earth-
 only fiction held its promise.

And the stage. Little boys with wooden swords,
we stabbed Caesar, clutched daggers, dressed as girls
dressed as boys, dressed as girls again,
sex buds blooming in our y-fronts,
voices breaking on pentameters
we wouldn't lose, no matter how
prosaic our afterlives. Our best teacher
beamed and applauded, his secret life
a frisson we couldn't know, could only feel.
God bless his solitude, his integrity,
his white leather suit on the Earl's Court Road.

So it went and goes on. I could write,
I discovered, could dazzle and blaze
and scream and puzzle and be praised.

So far so good. But will it last?

APPLAUSE, KING LEAR

a woman in her father's arms,
a semi-circle of numb disbelief;
all that thunder silenced,
not even a sprinkle of small rain.
Life stretched out, buried,
time an irrelevance;
fingertips close, averted eyes.

Then, at last, a crescendo of applause,
a way out, brotherhood of grief,
amazement. No further harm,
we pray, we trust. Violence
no more, agony shed
like an old skin. Only a rigid dance,
an empty space, abeyance of lies.

SUFFER

At last a light touch in a Russian tune,
a ragtime dance: doesn't tear your heart,
lay siege to your eardrums, drown you in a swell
mountain deep, gulag endless, vodka deadly.

Their very names bark with pleuritic pangs:
Glazunov, Scriabin, Shostakovich,
you sense it'll be a rough ride long before
the maestro lifts his revolver. My god

it was tough, it was history none of us
could imagine, let alone endure.
So it's amazing when humour breaks through,
when the song is gentle, erotic, replete.

If life is a labour camp, then art
dreams paradise against stupendous odds,
the climb is vertical, outcome uncertain
or certainly fatal. Brave souls play the fool.

BACK TO NATURE?

1. I stood upright in the old orchard,
dappled in rusty sunlight,
seeded the grass,
climbed into my concertinaed trousers
strolled back for afternoon tea.
Little Peters did not grow
in that quiet corner of the artists' retreat
and I did not try the trick again,
but creativity cannot always
create. We may leave skeins of life
on dying trees; we may revive.

2. Three jetties into Lake Bassenthwaite,
three young men under the tell-tale stars
sure only that it felt screaming good
to plunge into zero, to run,
apprentice Bacchantes,
drunk on hot sweet tea and friendship,
closer to themselves than all
the bright futures they did not believe.

Fly away, Peter, fly away Francis,
fly away Julius. Nets of learning await,
deep freeze the moonlight in description.

3. Not kitted out for the brambled headland,
hotfoot weary after the leaping faun
he'd tumbled and tasted all morning
he did, at last, fail; she called, lay down, opened,
careless of purple thorn and yellow gorse.
Jane Austen came to his rescue,
fully clothed in pelisse and bonnet:
'down there's where Louisa Musgrove fell'
And that was that. To this day,
he owes her reckless love,
his last, living breath.

DANCING ON DIFFERENT SHORES

Stave the First *for an unknown couple and Kay*

I saw a condom on the beach at Ferragudo,
it curled like ribbon kelp, milky yellow
and I wondered how cold it would be at night,
whether the lovers loved and still loved,
would I meet them without knowing, she in a rush,
twelve hours to face in a packed restaurant,
he ashamed of nowhere to go, empty wallet,
patched jeans?
Recalled the marram grass at Portrush,
cloudless skies, moonlight on your bare neck:
 the deep down sadness at the heart of things
broke me into crystal splinters, I was glad
to be this unlikely romantic, ablaze,
at a distance from the closest we'd been
could ever be, unsheathed, inside each other.

Stave the Second *for Dyna*

We'd let the children pelt along the strand
as we unpacked the Waitrose picnic:
nothing less than perfect for this lost week end.
The cottage like a landed naval hulk,
rickety ladders into the loft,
galley decked with bottles of Rioja,
an artichoke your wedding bouquet,

John Coltrane spinning on an old turntable:
My Favourite Things, Funny Valentine.
In the distance, sun painted the cliffs pink,
lights began to cluster the hillside town

The magic trio trailed back, tar and seaweed
bearded their snazzy yellow wellingtons;
the girls egged each other into gurning,
Jamie danced towards them, an ogre,
a jackanapes, a bundle of laughter.
Drained by indecision, blind enough
to sense this couldn't last, we made love
at once illicit and elated. My nerve
failed, your pride kept anguish unpacked
until the rain -drenched drive to separate homes.

Stave the Third *for Lisa, forever*

Our turn to play the fool, drenched trousers,
icy toes, breathless scrambles up the cliffside,
clutching at thistles on sandstone striations;
like gods or aliens or stone age monkeys
we tread, marvel, link hands and let go.
We have long since ceased to sing, but know
no better than this, silhouettes in flesh,
memory of memories, breathing shades,
rock pool conquistadors, dancers on the edge,
a world into and away from ourselves.

My love scares you, you say. I understand,
mourn my incontinence, my jealous rage,
 every minute you spend elsewhere.
Happiness suppressed, forever postponed,
how can we bear it? Schubert's late sonatas,
wordless, sublime, unrecognised. They will do.
A marriage of dissonant minds, cadence
without issue, absolute as the last note.

BLOOD RED MOON

yet another thing to take on trust:
somewhere in the world a pink grapefruit,
a gouged eye. Not here. We climbed the highest point,
swaddled in cloud. Lightning gashed the hill sides,
spotlit steeples and chimneys for a second.
This was worth seeing, but was it worth
going to see? It felt special, certainly,
shoulder to shoulder with a dozen people,
quiet as choir boys sipping the altar wine.
That was it, then: no revelation,
no inter stellar sighs of wonder,
 perspectives from the other side. Only
a sense of being small, of a void
we had not the skill or serenity
to penetrate. Other pilgrims climbed
as we descended, we swapped platitudes
to gulp back embarrassment. Astonished
by the backcloth of rolling sea, looming sky
and no clear division, this was worship
of a different order than we'd imagined,
as if a church we would never visit
rose up in our minds, a stone cross,
not for sacrifice, but for endless praise:
we are more than the sum of our parts
and less than we have been led to believe.

BEES AND CANDLES

1.

My daughter, nine years old, Notre Dame,
a small giant under those bright circles,
those gaunt, bony vaults;
she turns her eyes towards a small, bare altar
picks a candle to light for Great Grandma,
that warm old lady all powder and perfume,
who'd bend for a kiss, get only a cheek,
whose rock cakes were a sugar crumble,
whose television was company,
whose lace curtains were a spy hole on the world.

As the candle burnt down, the prayer rose:
'I don't want Grandpa to die'. That would suffice,
were he to go the next day. Being loved,
that's more than half the story,
feeds a flame that will not gutter,
outlasts all cathedrals
ruined or remaining.

2.

Judy was a kind of candle,
  flesh and calico, ran screaming
down threadbare carpets,
  doused by a flatmate.
Crisped and flayed, they raced her body
through city streets, her heartbeat
a broken music, a flicker.

Only her face escaped immolation,
she surfaced like a mermaid,
sang and sang for her life:
sings still. Miracles are very hard work,
each year the candle of grace
consumes itself, slow and sure,
sheds light on yet another
dark corner.

3. *'come, build in the empty house of the stare' (Yeats)*

That long back garden, fringed with lilac,
lavender, poppies, wide eyed sunflowers,
wisteria on the red brick wall,
so briefly in bloom. Sweet things
happen in Huddersfield, swarms of black bees
make their homes in the Pennine damp,
exotic refugees in stripy pyjamas,
sipping and flitting from stamen to stigma.
We shall build hive after hive
in England's not always pleasant land,
led gently by the Pied Piper of pollen,
Professor Riyad from Damascus.
We shall fill our cells with light and life
until peace returns for Syria,
until we learn to honour ourselves
for giving sanctuary, bless the chance
to give blessing. To be humankind
is our birthright, death to deny it.

I'M READY FOR MY CLOSE UP, MR. DE MILLE

It's been hazy as hell round here:
we stumble and sniff our ways,
much like poor old Gloucester; unlike him,
I do not think we see better,
being blind. It's the anonymity
appeals, we loom out of the mist,
tramp steamers selling whatever
we've laid our hands on. Don't get me wrong,
there's drama in the grainy drizzle,
you seem miles away across the field
as I skirt the barbed wire fence
and a lost lamb bleats like a foghorn.

As a child I'd scoot from lamp post
to lamp post, swathed in yellow clouds,
an outlaw between the worlds
I couldn't quite fit, a lone ranger
on his make believe grey stallion,
a myth of my own making.
Then, as now, I coughed my way to stardom.

The real one also lurks in the shadows,
tumbles down dreamscapes, sinks into
the ineluctable ocean
from which there is no message,
only the skirl of ancient pipes
and her voice, a siren, a saint,
talking to someone else after all.

I AM A TIBETAN BUDDHIST,

live in Walthamstow,
keep cats and a wolverine.

today I killed as few creatures
as possible. It was necessary
to modify my own Karma,
so I swung on by the lap dancing club;
topped off the day by topping myself.

The flowers on the wall
are deep fried plastic,
the letters scramble off the page,
an army of literate ants.

My enemies have soft voices,
they feed me chocolate,
hit on my woman
and finish my sentences for me.

INARTICULATE SPEECH OF THE HEART, OR
HOW KARLOWICZ WROTE ABOUT HIS FRIEND'S
SUICIDE

Rage, mostly, a brooding, bruised sky,
then the swirling waters of a mill pond,
the deep drop. An arctic silence,
broken only by the crack of glaciers,
the wide wings of the Albatross
whistle of the North Wind in the ghost ship.

The perfect brevity of wisteria;
some long conversation touching topics
way beyond their grasp. A boy's kite,
loaded with wishes; a map marked
from home to a high place and back.
A snarl from an unplayed electric guitar.

Then and last and forever, guilt.
He had not said, but said so much
as Karlowicz sank into his own frenzy,
that absolute ignorance we wear
as a safety net. *Beyond help.*
Sounds like rain: dry, scorching, toxic rain.

CROWS AND CHIMPANZEES ARE OF EQUAL INTELLIGENCE

Not a surprise; crows imagine,
act beyond the instant .They wait.
Chimps, of course, contemplate,
gaze through the bars at cretins,
pick fleas from each other in love.
Their indignities are vile
and myriad. But they were saved one.
Ted Hughes left well alone.

Here is the real song of the crow:

Kraa. Just clearing my voice.
We do, we admit, survive,
thrive, in unlikely places.
On a motorway, spearing guts
and flesh, soaring high
as great metal boxes hurtle
towards us. Hunched in bare branches
like cryptograms with no meaning.

What we are not is symbolic;
post apocalyptic. Sick.
We do not represent
the morbid egotism
of a self styled avatar,
a Yorkshire monolith
a mythopoeic monster
crowned in Belladonna.

Had you noticed how we
adapt? How, sometimes, we flock,
sometimes lurk solo? Way back,
before metaphors stalked the earth,
we reigned with fish and turtles,
snakes and blazing eyes in the sky.
We are messengers of ourselves,
crow, kraa, korr. No translation.

THE LAMB WHO WATCHED TELEVISION AND THE COW WHO GOT IN A MOOD.

I don't know, but I think he nuzzled the screen,
found glassy cold and not woolly flesh;
as for Biscuit, the Jersey cow,
it may have been the wind, or the tractor's growl
or it may have been Bob's great fat neck,
not the most inviting sight for a girl
too shy to even shit in public.
Bob's the bull; and I made up the other bit
like we make up almost everything
about animals, especially homo sapiens.
Not that I think we are not sapiens,
not that I think we do not share more than the earth
with our fabulous hard done by relatives.
Hunger. Sex. Terror. A dream life so complex
that God must be as incomprehensible
as Proust, as many layered as a crinoline.

If I had the key to all metaphors
I should tell you and together
we would transform our patchwork love
into a perfect crystal, a tree of life,
a stream entirely its own shape, flowing
into the sea that is ice and fire
and forever.
In the meantime, I shall watch with the lamb
and you may sulk in the corner of the field.

TRIPADVISOR

This veggie café's seen better days,
although it's only just opened.
Festooned with flowers, like Lear
on the blasted heath, she who sips soup
engages whoever she might
with a slack line or a smile.
It's not me this time, my visor's down,
but two dressed for the Himalayas
who gain the benefit of mung beans
by proxy. In a corner,
Hiawatha's mum peruses
eighty ancient remedies,
washed down with green tea in a brown mug.

Depressions not on the menu,
it is the menu, the scrubbed pine tables,
the garish flyers promising new,
renewable life, eighty quid a throw.
Who'd want to save the planet
for this little lot, this vault of piety,
this congregation of singular souls?
I would. I love the obsolete,
the conformity of the odd.
This is a dating agency
for the dated and I shall come again
and leave alone, like all the rest.

ONE OF THE BEST.

For the inimitable Jude Alderson

You wore a tiny dress in silver sequins,
every neurotic nancy boy's secret love,
androgynous angel, stiletto sharp;
I swanked about in a silk dressing gown,
deliberately obtuse, doing my best
to be noticed in anonymity.
Swallowed my amazement to find you alone
In the chill night-time, to walk you home,
to hear us both chuck words into the air,
little caring how they'd land. Held you close,
like a poem that shivered through my other-
ness. Felt the wild sanity of the moon
and laughed like I'd only ever laughed in dreams.

Somehow the truth of all that make believe
does not fade; and I know that what they call
the real world is a sad, shifting fiction.
Sing to me at seventeen, at seventy:
I'll do my best, in my odd way
to echo your call.

ELEGY FOR MANKIND AT THE SEA SIDE

the black backed gulls soar so high and wild
this morning; they could have machine guns
poised on their pinions, it may be time
for revenge. This land was their land
to sow with shit, to strut, to command
like alabaster statues in the sea mist.
Dive bombers in main street might improve matters,
cull the dingy cafes, sad charity shops,
 fish and chips imported from Norway.
Empires and thrones and dominions fall
as cliffs crumble, songs peddle nostalgia,
poets tart up vacuity with ground-
breaking imitations of alien forms
or txt thier whey into the harts of yoof,
 limbo along to foul mouthed doggerel
.

It may, indeed be time. The rainbow's promise,
the sermon on the mount, the great gift
of life itself: can Homo Sapiens
really be said to have held his side
of the bargain? Worse still, there was no bargain,
we have screwed it up totally without threat
or promise. If you seek a monument,
look around. Then go for a viscous coffee
in Kath's Kitchen. Whatever you do,
don't look up.

A BIRD THAT SINGS ON AND ON,
LATE INTO THE SEASON,
IS PROBABLY A LONELY BACHELOR
WHO HAS FAILED TO ATTRACT A MATE

at sixty seven I must count
as one of the last old songbirds
on the branch. Embarrassment
doesn't come into it, nor the stale
repetition of the moonstruck lyrics;
no audience required, I guess
I'd do myself a mischief

if anyone answered the call,
these ragged feathers'd spiral away
in the chill wind. No, I do not
demand payment or reciprocation,
can manage catcalls and indifference
with equal aplomb. But it is
a grim business, being a blast
beruffled rusty blackbird on a stump.
There is no rhyme or reason
to my monotone anthem,
no urgent message nor haunted
lament. It simply is, as it was
when I began, a smudge on the page
a thin insistent yodel, scaring
 young girls with an intensity
that scarcely knew itself.
A lonely bachelor doesn't
even touch on the true desolation
that spins this long player
into eternity and back again.
I can't catch the voice I boomerang
out of the air into the darkness.

THE STRANGELY VACANT GAZE OF THE FISHMONGER'S WIFE

Does not catch my attention because I like
my women on a slab, not does it speak
homesickness for the glad girl she was
all those years before he landed her
in that fishy light.
          It's more that she floats,
like a love song by The Doors, that she belongs
in strawberry fields, in a swirling kaftan;
no one notices she is a queen of cool
in a bloody overall. She dishes out
commiserations alongside the fresh crab,
the flattened kippers, she looks on the bright side
with a small sigh. My Spanish Caravan
is not parked in the High Street, nor do my poems
conjure salty flavours in her mind.
But I do try, little by little, to edge
between the woman at the counter
and the buccaneers we both might have been.
Who do I think I'm looking at, strangely vacant?

I'VE JUST HEARD RICHARD RODNEY BENNET PLAY 'THE MAN I LOVE'

and I'm struck by the way it fits like a glove,
his slick fingers glide over the keys,
settle for a second, then rise in joy
and mischief. O how often I'd wish
love went like that, minds and bodies
married in the moment, sent into the world
stronger and smiling, private music
made public. Nothing counted, nothing
costed: ecstatic and still, like the night.

A PENNY FOR THEM

the child in the wellies knows no more
who she is than the dragon fly tells the time
or the rock feels itself falling;
she casts a reflection,
like the mustard sun, like her mind.

O do not hurry, small one,
there are faces to make aplenty
there will be days you do not wish for,
voices far from your own.

ice may not chill, loneliness may not
appall your regiment of one;
but for now, hands in your pockets,
no particular place to go
I fear for your perfect beauty,
your body planted on this plot of earth.
Live to tell your story as our parents
charted theirs in the inscrutable stars.

NOTHING IS THAT FUNNY (FOR GERALD)

those are not all laughter lines.
Like a pitiless artist, time
carves its folds and contours
in your face. Makes you human,
you tell yourself, each groove
a small odyssey. Pain is beautiful,
a lament by the waters of Babylon,
a suitcase packed for separation.

It's when you're puffed up with fear,
a fish cornered among the fish,
when you are so ugly
your enemies spit you out,
disgusted, that's when a nail
driven deep into your neck
is the only way. And you flop
to the floor, a burst balloon,

a pool of undigested plankton,
a stench. A bit late to re-define;
then again, you wrote your memoirs
at seven, were buried at thirty,
resurrected through a tube.
The jigsaw puzzle's blue all over,
there is no horizon, not a tree;
there's a blot of yellow. Where does that go?

2.

A quartet of actors in a playing field:
they are Pyramus and Thisbe,
they are Nick Bottom and Francis Flute,
they are an acrobatic leap
into loving arms. Table cloth picnics,
teenagers on bikes keeping their distance,
enthralled, not saying so. Above,
a cluster of bright balloons,
tagged with messages; they fight upwards,
hopeful as tadpoles. They may make it.
Most will not. We should crowd the skies,
scale the heavens with all we'd wish for,
all we'd never get by landing on the moon,
by searching for the wrong door. It's time
to step out of time running out,
 to shed those tired feathers and start again.
We are below you, hands outstretched:
unless you dare to fall, you will never rise.
 Better to die in the wind than live in a box.

HIDDEN SHALLOWS

you swank into the room
like Lester Piggott on Derby Day;
they admire the way you don't notice
their adulation. Star quality.

The figure in the playground,
the pile of rags in the empty station,
the cry of a gannet; the forgotten.
Here is your nonchalance, your pool of piss.

Every inch a king, he who gives all
because he owns nothing. The husk,
the seed. Perhaps you chose this plot,
perhaps it chose you. Carry on

regardless.

LITTLE BOXES

our last box, at least, a hexagon;
better still, a casket, a wicker creel.

Anything but a square, fashioned not to fit
anything human. A stamp, a cell,
an enclosure that clearly defines, grades,
disposes once and for all, a corral.

I am bloody odd, bits of me poke out,
I cannot answer questions in boxes.
On a scale of one to ten how do you feel?
'Minus one now, eleven before you asked,
settling to somewhere between the two.'

I drive in a box I live in a box
on top of another box, I tick a box
to contact the love of my life. I keep
tears in boxes, let them out at night
when they will cause less din and discomfort.

My favourite box contains cyanide,
the complete works of Jonathan Swift
a self-detonating stink bomb
and all my most embarrassing moments.

If you fence me in I shall square up to you
in the boxing ring, beat you to a straight line,
corner you and your wife in a love triangle
and suck honey out of your tessellation.

I mean business. Have the key to box thirteen.

MELANCHOLIA

you'd say it was a formless mass
lurking deep in the silt of the ocean,
shifting on its hams. Lying await.
Starlings circle around the spot, avoid it.

It knows me inside out, mimics
the march of my little army,
attacks when I most require defence,
The story is always in abeyance,

There is no ever after but no ending,
Scraps and fragments under glass,
labels and dates, futile, risible.
The best I can wish is to pass.

Bob up. Bob up and float. Grin,
bare it. Spend a fortune
on the trick cyclist, simply to discover
paranoia to be true, in minute detail.

Ahab, the white whale, Ishmael,
the albatross, the cross, the nought,
the rusty harpoon that doubles
as a fountain pen of great beauty,

makes its mark. I would not deny
my monster, would not feed it,
let it feed on me. Since, after all,
there is no choice. The sea bed,
the sea's voice.

I MET A TRAVELLER FROM A MODERN LAND

well, Norwich. She was in blue boots, ski jacket,
she picked her way along the glistering sand,
wondered how freezing was the water. I glowed,
enthused, bullied. *This is a piece of cake,*
I averred. On cue, the sun burnt through,
we continued our colloquy, flirting
in that fabulous way you know nothing
will happen. Hinted at hidden lovers,
like tattooes under our shirts. I had no shirt,
so my label lurked elsewhere, my mythic brand.

      For we belong to no one, we are not slaves,
we swim, stand, talk alone, return to our nests
where we might swive and sweat, Venus and Mars
caught in a golden net.

      It is good to be grandiose,
it satisfies for a moment. Allows the day
to blaze and fade, me to fold my towel,
she to gather shells, to dip her toes
in the bevelled lace of the breakers.

      I would not write our names on the sand,
not because they will be erased, but because
this is better, this *we shall not meet again.*
Search along the coast for the song of the snipe,
that's what you came for. That beak of his
writes a history only John Clare
could indite, wild, whirling, like a child.

How may we say we have lost someone,
lost something, when we do not know
where we are? Only a smoking gun

fixes us to the spot, freezes us slow
and quicksilver in the last minute.
'Go', whispers the dragon fly, 'go now.'

It is to our cost, our very high cost
we stretch our palms towards the light,
surrender beneath our own paper cross.

AGES OF UNCERTAINTY

1. Screen Killers

so tedious, this ferocity. A woman strides
out of the smog, high heel boots,
a swirling black skirt. Her eyes fix forwards
and we quake. She devours a young man
like a sprat, smokes cigarillos,
chews rattlesnakes. Oh for Marlene,
a touch of wit, a petticoat,
something for the boys in the back room

Hitler happened and they had to laugh;
we take ourselves seriously,
face bubble gum villains. Who gives
a flying fuck about method acting?
The lies we live are the real thing.

2. Que Sais Je?

There is a limit to diffidence.
I know full well the idiot in me,
the gang we contrive. We call a spade
a shovel, do not suffer fools gladly,
are infinitely complacent. Go away
yelled the aborigines, we do not
desire your trinkets, your smoking guns.
A criminal civilisation settled,
scum on the clear pool. Second chances
come at a price, dream time over.
No sooner do we belong
but we turn away the stranger. I know
what I know. I know my enemy
smiles, lools a lot like me.

3. The Yawning Chasm of the Open Mind

Once upon a time the tortoise
upped sticks and sought an elsewhere.
Didn't much matter where it was,
the change was all that counted.
Parked on the M!. One place
is pretty much like another.
We become the past tense,
leave an impression:
lover, lunatic, brother.
I know who I am. I'm not that.

DANCE MUSIC

they danced on the wards with holes in their lungs,
knew euphoria with dying breath.

A plant turns towards the bright side,
having grown in the dark. I walk a garden
I'd walked as a young man, Dylan Thomas to hand,
or Charlotte or Sheila or devastation.
Anywhere to be be nowhere
away from home.
                Now it is my daughter,
her daughters, those marble Naiads stretching
towards another autumn, an evening
that will not pass.
                And I pass on,
confident these lovely girls, these women
are not marble and so they will hurt
and yet they will always have a home
in each other and I may have helped
them make and find the place from which they may soar
as I fumble with my notebook, take a picture
in syllables and confess, not for the last time
I have no choice but to seek the wrong words
in the right order or the right words
in the wrong order and be not afraid
that I repeat myself like an old man's gut.

The time to soar is not yet. Time to dance,
orange squash in a blue plastic beaker,
Guy's Hospital. Three men out of twelve died
as I was demoted from the Nurse's station,
bed by bed. The opposite of faith
is certainty. I believe we may ride
the wind, do not know how. Love
gathers around the mortal ring
and we are roses, we are family.

HARP CRAFT

I threw myself a scrap of paper,
it was all I could eat,
I'd choked on daily bread,
sensible shoes, the astonishing
and the banal. Sought deprivation
so that I may mark the streaks of dusky pink,
the tumbles of cloud. For appetite palls,
I damn the familiar as I damn myself,
Mephistopheles at the station,
impatient to leave, reluctant to arrive,
knowing I must not start here
if I wish to end up there.

I recall the instant, the bright sense of freedom,
the gash, the gasp of delight.
 I also recall the recall, the music,
the heartache graffiti that led me,
 left me here, afraid of more and less.

I hear today that Jessye Norman is dead,
that magniicent spirit, that inside out voice;
I dwell in her defiance:
'pigeonholimg only pleases pigeons'
and I'm glad to over alliterate.
It is where we began amd I turn
back to the blank scraps, to the pause
where harpsong lies. Love the evening blood red,
the morning blaze. Know that my shirts on the line
send a message there is no need to translate,
as blithe and futile and urgent as a poem.

AUDENESQUE

I don't spare myself, so I don't spare you,
though you must have to dissociate,
like a surgeon, like an executioner.
You must. Why I shall never know.

Meantime I count the bricks, tick off the dates,
walk and walk; black out the clocks,
aspire to the Sufic condition,
much like you I guess, but with no choice.

at last, underwater, I find a cavern
where pearls eye the kingdom,
grace the seabed. I do not belong,
but visit, grateful, in your arms.

DEAREST LORD, WHEN WILL I DIE?

(cantata 8, Johann Sebastian Bach)

I'm in no special hurry; simply wished
to check in, see if your plans
differed in any way from mine.

First of all, I'd like to keep a pig;
to see the Northern Lights;
to fuse sex and feelings
in a firework display
that leaves our bodies intact.

To trip down The Spanish Steps
with granddaughter one,
watch her fill her spirit
with Keats and Shelley
then drive off in a Porsche.

To be sat in the front row
when granddaughter two
throws Torvald's manuscript
on the fire. Is Hedda
through and through. Herselves.

To secure- in other words
for you to promise-
happiness and health
to the women who love me.
All two of them

Failing all that, it's no deal,
I shall be content to pootle
on, centuries of bad jokes
and small satisfactions...
The choice is yours, Big Man.

This makes no less sense
than your secret contract.
Dearest Lord, trust me, as I trust You